FIGHTING TO SURVIVE UNDERGROUND
TERRIFYING TRUE STORIES

by Nancy Dickmann

COMPASS POINT BOOKS
a capstone imprint

Fighting to Survive is published by
Compass Point Books, an imprint of Capstone.
1710 Roe Crest Drive, North Mankato, Minnesota 56003
www.capstonepub.com

**Library of Congress Cataloging-in-Publication Data is available on the Library
of Congress website**

ISBN: 978-0-7565-6427-8 (hardcover)
ISBN: 978-0-7565-6567-1 (paperback)
ISBN: 978-0-7565-6428-5 (ebook pdf)

Summary: Describes the terrifying true stories of people who survived being trapped
underground for extended periods of time.

Editorial Credits
Aaron J. Sautter, editor; Terri Poburka, designer; Morgan Walters, media researcher;
Kathy McColley, production specialist

Photo Credits
Associated Press:Dale Sparks, 25; Getty Images: Barbara Laing, 10, David Woo, 12,
Fairfax Media, 33, Ian Waldie, 29, New York Daily News Archive, 23, William Nation,
7; Newscom: El Mercurio/ZUMAPRESS, 41, Felipe Trueba/EFE, 47, Gary Gardiner/
EyePush Newsphotos, 15, HUGO INFANTE/UPI, 46, POOL/REUTERS, 20, 34, 45,
STR/REUTERS, 43; Shutterstock: 24Novembers, 5, AridOcean, 6, DAAgius, 57, Ethan
Daniels, 55, Isaac Marzioli, design element throughout, King Ropes Access, 17, Mark
Agnor, 30, Miloje, design element throughout, pavalena, 14, 36, Peter Hermes Furian,
49, Rainer Lesniewski, 27, scubadesign, 52, trabantos, 58, Valerijs Novickis, 50, Vitalii
Nesterchuk, Cover, xpixel, design element throughout; Wikimedia: Eigenes Werk, 37,
US Occupational Safety and Health Administration, 18

Printed and bound in the USA.
PA99

TABLE OF
CONTENTS

INTRODUCTION

Earth's surface is an amazing place. It's covered with dense forests, hot deserts, tall mountains, and deep oceans. But it's just as interesting below the surface. Dig deep enough, and you might find the remains of ancient animals or civilizations. There are natural wonders too. Caves can spread for miles below the ground. Some caverns are barely big enough to squeeze through, while others are the size of a cathedral. Earth also has underground rivers, pockets of natural gas, and melted rock.

EXPLORING UNDERGROUND

People have been exploring this underground world for thousands of years. Prehistoric people in Spain and France painted cave walls to show their culture. In addition to exploring natural caves, ancient people also dug deep into the earth. The ancient Romans mined copper, tin, lead, and gold. These metals were used to make coins, weapons, jewelry, and pipes for carrying water. Other ancient civilizations also dug complex mines.

With modern technology, miners are able to dig deep through layers of hard rock. Divers also use high-tech breathing equipment to explore underwater caves. But even with modern technology, people have only explored a fraction of what is there. We live on Earth's crust—the outermost layer of the planet. The crust ranges from 3 to 25 miles (5 to 40 kilometers) thick. The deepest hole humans ever dug made it only about halfway through the crust.

BURIED DANGERS

Traveling deep underground can be dangerous. The deeper you go, the hotter it gets. The air pressure also increases. Tunnels can easily flood as water seeps through the rocks. Mining uses heavy machinery and sometimes explosives. Both can trigger rockfalls and cave-ins. Caves can be especially dangerous. Some are like huge mazes. If something goes wrong deep in a flooded passageway, it can be a very long way out.

The people who travel underground know that they're taking risks. They do their best to prepare for anything that can go wrong. But accidents still happen. The people in this book have all faced deadly situations underground—but they were all lucky enough to survive.

THE GIRL IN THE WELL
JESSICA MCCLURE

October 14, 1987, started off as a normal day in Midland, Texas. This medium-sized city was a center of oil and gas production. It was also once the hometown of President George H. W. Bush. But within days, Midland would quickly become a household name. People everywhere were gripped by the incredible story of Cissy and Chip McClure and their 18-month-old daughter, Jessica.

IN THE BLINK OF AN EYE

That day little Jessica McClure was playing happily with four other children. She was in the backyard with her mother at her aunt Jamie's house. When the phone rang in the house, Cissy went to answer it. She wasn't inside for more than a couple of minutes when she and Jamie suddenly heard screams from the backyard. The two women raced outside to see what had happened. The rest of the children were still there, but Jessica was nowhere to be seen. She seemed to have vanished into thin air.

It was a few frantic moments before Cissy realized what had happened. She remembered that there was an old well in the backyard. Its narrow 8-inch (20-centimeter) wide shaft led deep underground. A large rock covered the opening to prevent any accidents. But somehow the well had gotten uncovered. And somehow Jessica had found the small hole and fallen into it.

CALLING FOR HELP

Cissy raced back into the house to phone for help. "I didn't know what to do," she later recalled. "I just ran in and called the police. They were there within three minutes, but it felt like a lifetime." Unfortunately, when the police arrived, there was little they could do. Jessica was wedged tightly in the narrow shaft, about 22 feet (7 meters) underground. Getting her out would be a long and tricky process. Her family could only hope that she would survive long enough for rescuers to reach her.

Baby Jessica McClure, with her parents Cissy (left) and Chip (right), after the accident in 1987

A DIFFICULT RESCUE

Police officer Bobbie Jo Hall was the first officer on the scene. She was horrified at what she found. The well was so narrow, and Jessica was so deep, that it seemed practically impossible to get her out. Cissy was panicking, terrified that Jessica would die. Hall called down the shaft to Jessica three or four times before finally hearing her cry in response. Although the situation was bad, at least Jessica was still alive. Hall lowered a flashlight hooked to a measuring tape into the well to see how deep the little girl was.

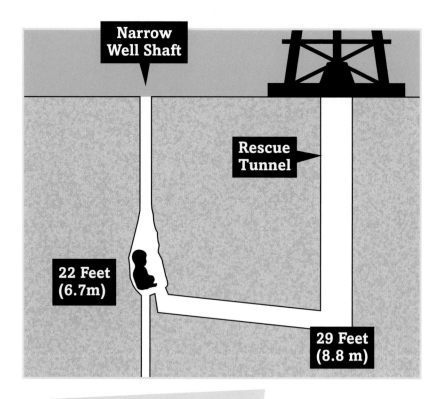

Narrow Well Shaft

Rescue Tunnel

22 Feet (6.7m)

29 Feet (8.8 m)

To rescue Jessica, workers had to drill a separate shaft nearby that was large enough for rescuers to fit through.

Jessica was tightly wedged in the well. In fact, she had ended up in a position similar to doing the splits, with her right leg stuck above her head. Even if she weren't so tightly stuck, she was too young to grab a rope and be pulled out.

HARD GROUND

Hall made several calls to get the equipment needed to rescue Jessica. Rescue workers had to tear down fences to get the rescue equipment into the backyard. At first, they tried digging with a backhoe. But after going down about 3 feet (1 m), they struck layers of solid rock. It would take heavy machinery—and a lot of skill—to reach Jessica.

The rescuers soon realized that the only way to get Jessica out was to drill another hole. It would be parallel to the well. Once they reached the required depth, they would have to tunnel sideways to reach the toddler. Luckily, thanks to Midland's oil and gas industry, there were plenty of people around with a lot of drilling experience.

Jessica's family looked on as a large team assembled to help with the rescue. A mining engineer flew in from New Mexico to manage the operation. Several oil drilling experts assisted him. Rescue workers, police officers, and paramedics also were on hand at all times. Friends and neighbors gathered to pray and watch the rescue efforts.

Workers lowered a microphone into the well to listen to Jessica. They heard her talking and even singing a song about Winnie the Pooh.

DRILLING DOWN

The drilling began using a rat-hole rig. This powerful machine was designed for planting telephone poles in the ground. The hole the rescuers drilled was about 30 inches (76 cm) wide. It took the rescuers about 6 hours to dig to a depth of about 29 feet (9 m). Then it was time to tunnel sideways to reach Jessica in the well. This was a much shorter distance, but it was a hard job and took much longer.

Rescuers took turns to work on the sideways shaft. First they were lowered into the new shaft, carrying a 45-pound (20-kilogram) jackhammer. Once in position, they lay on their stomachs and punched out the rock between small holes that had been drilled. It was slow work—about one inch per hour.

KEEPING JESSICA SAFE

The rescuers were working as fast as they could, but they also had to be careful. Drilling through solid rock and using jackhammers created a lot of vibration. They had to take care not to cause any damage to the well. They didn't want to put Jessica in any more danger.

Throughout the rescue operation, workers pumped oxygen into the well for Jessica to breathe. They kept calling out and talking to her to make sure she was all right. They had lowered microphones next to her inside the well so they could hear her crying or talking. At one point they lowered a video camera and got a side view of her.

THE WORLD WATCHES

As the rescue efforts progressed, television crews gathered. Jessica's incredible ordeal had caught the nation's imagination. The rescue was covered live by CNN, the only 24-hour news channel in the country. Across the United States, millions of people—including President Ronald Reagan—watched and waited to hear if the little girl would be saved. The story was covered as far away as Germany, China, and Brazil. Complete strangers sent Jessica's family cards, flowers, and toys.

FREE AT LAST

On the evening of October 16, 1987, paramedic Robert O'Donnell wriggled down into the new shaft. He was chosen for the job because of his slender build. On TV screens in every state, people watched in amazement. O'Donnell emerged from the well into the glare of the spotlights, carrying Baby Jessica. She was bruised, scraped, and wrapped in gauze—but she was alive and safe.

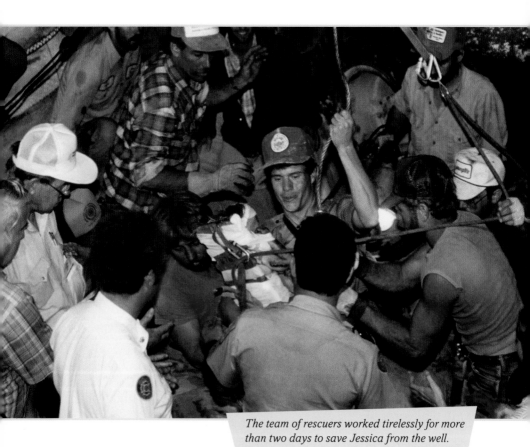

The team of rescuers worked tirelessly for more than two days to save Jessica from the well.

Paramedics raced to help Jessica. After such a long time without food and water, she was hungry and dehydrated. But there was a much bigger concern. The whole time she was in the well, her right leg was above her head. This position had cut off some of the blood flow, and she had developed gangrene. The tissues of her foot had effectively died. Some doctors wanted to amputate her foot, but others were determined to try to save it. After several surgeries, they managed to use skin from her hip to reconstruct her foot. The only thing they couldn't save was her pinkie toe.

Jessica also had wounds on her forehead and the back of her head. These were caused when she rested her head against the side of the well. The vibrations from the drilling had split the skin. The wounds left her with a scar on her forehead and a bald patch on the back of her head.

CELEBRITY

Jessica's ordeal had turned her into an overnight celebrity. Vice President George H. W. Bush was in the middle of running for president. He had a busy schedule, but he still took time to visit her in the hospital. However, Jessica slept through his whole visit! After recovering, she later got to meet Bush—who was now president—and his wife, Barbara. In the meantime, donations poured in from people across the country. They paid for all of Jessica's hospital care, and there was enough left over to set up a trust fund for her. Producers made a movie about her rescue. And the well? It was filled in with cement, with a metal lid inscribed with the words "For Jessica 10-16-87, with love from all of us."

POISONED AIR
RANDAL MCCLOY

Inside Earth's crust are many minerals and other useful substances. People have dug into the crust to mine for coal, copper, gold, and other minerals for thousands of years. Beneath the Appalachian Mountains in the eastern United States, several mines produce coal for burning in power plants. Coal mines employ thousands of workers—but it can be a dangerous job.

BACK TO WORK

On the morning of January 2, 2006, workers were arriving at a mine in Sago, West Virginia. They were returning to work after a break for the holidays. The Sago mine extended more than 2.5 miles (4 km) into the coal-rich hills. Although it was only a few hundred feet underground, coal miners knew that their job was risky. A few years earlier, nine coal miners had been trapped in a flooded mine in Pennsylvania for 77 hours before being

Sago Coal Mine Explosion

rescued. But early that morning, a fire boss at the Sago mine declared that it was safe. Shortly before 6:30 a.m., two crews headed into the mine to start work. The miners travelled into the mine on a mantrip, a train-like vehicle that runs on rails.

Sago coal mine near Buckhannon, West Virginia

EXPLOSION!

The two crews headed for two sections known as "One Left" and "Two Left." Two Left was the mine's most distant working point, and One Left came just before it. The Two Left crew was several minutes ahead of foreman Owen Jones and the One Left crew. Then, about 6:30 a.m., a huge explosion ripped through the mine.

To this day, no one is certain what caused the explosion. A flammable gas called methane occurs naturally within coal mines. If a pocket of methane had built up in the mine, a single spark could have been enough to ignite it. At the time the miners were beginning their shift, there was a huge thunderstorm in Sago. It's possible that lightning provided the spark to trigger the explosion.

CHAOS AND PANIC

Whatever the cause, the effects of the explosion were devastating. Thick black smoke and fumes filled the mine tunnels. There were 14 men on the mantrip heading for One Left. They weren't very far into the mine. Even so, the explosion blew off some of the workers' helmets. Luckily, the men had a clear path to safety. But what had happened to the 12 men of the Two Left crew? They had traveled farther into the mine.

Unfortunately, the Two Left crew's mantrip had passed the point where the explosion took place. They were now trapped. Owen Jones' brother Jesse was part of that crew, and Jones decided to go in and look for the crewmembers. But first he had to convince the rest of his crew to get to safety, rather than helping him. Jones and a few other men traveled as far into the mine as they could before they had to stop.

They carried detectors that tested whether the air was safe enough to breathe. The detectors showed that the mine had unsafe levels of carbon monoxide. This deadly gas is common in coal mines, especially in places with poor ventilation. It's produced by the exhaust of mining vehicles, as well as by the coal itself. High levels of carbon monoxide are also common after a methane explosion inside a coal mine. The explosion ignites any coal dust in the air. The coal dust burns, but without enough oxygen, it doesn't burn completely. This process creates even more carbon monoxide.

Jones and the others decided they had to stop. Without specialized breathing equipment, they couldn't go any farther.

Mine workers use gas detectors to learn if the air inside the mine is safe to breathe.

DID YOU KNOW?

Carbon monoxide is an invisible gas with no smell or taste. When you breathe it, it enters your bloodstream. The gas mixes with red blood cells, making them unable to carry oxygen through the body. At low levels, carbon monoxide can cause dizziness, tiredness, and shortness of breath. At high levels, it can be deadly.

TRAPPED

Deep inside the mine, the Two Left crewmembers knew they were in a bad situation. Martin Toler, the foreman, quickly took charge. At first, the men tried to ride to safety on their mantrip, but debris blocked the tracks. They might have been able to get around the debris on foot, but the smoke filling the mine was too thick to see a path. The crew all reached for their "self-rescuers." These pieces of breathing equipment provided one hour of emergency oxygen. The miners hoped that would be enough time to get to safety.

But four of the miners couldn't get their self-rescuers to work. One of them, Jerry Groves, was standing near Randal McCloy Jr. McCloy was 26 years old and the youngest member of the crew. He did his best to get Groves' self-rescuer working, but he couldn't.

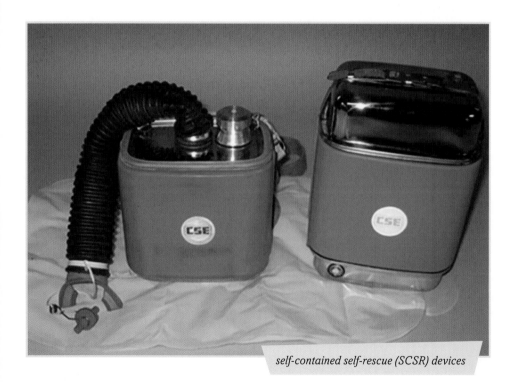

self-contained self-rescue (SCSR) devices

Instead, he shared his air supply with Groves. Among the rest of the crew, those with air also shared with those who didn't have any. That emergency breathing equipment was critically important. Aside from the thick smoke inside the mine, the carbon monoxide level was dangerously high.

FINDING SAFETY

The miners had been trained on what to do in an emergency. In fact, inside each of their helmets was a sticker with a safety reminder. It told them to set up plastic sheet barricades to keep out dust and then listen for sounds of rescue. They then should pound on the metal bolts in the ceiling to let rescuers know where they were. After resting for 15 minutes, they should start pounding again.

Toler, McCloy, and the other miners followed the procedure. They took turns using a sledgehammer to pound on the bolts. The effort left them gasping for breath in the poor air. And they couldn't hear any sign that rescuers could hear them.

After pounding on the bolts, the 12 miners retreated to the coalface. This was the farthest part of the mine, where coal was still being dug. It was 2.5 miles (4 km) from the mine entrance. But it was the farthest they could get from the thick smoke in the main tunnel. There they set up a barricade of plastic sheeting. Its purpose was to give the men a safe space away from the harmful gases where they could wait for rescue.

ON THE SURFACE

Rescue teams were gathering at the mine entrance. The miners' worried family members were arriving too. By this point it was more than four hours since the explosion, but rescuers hadn't yet gone into the mine. Officials were worried that there might be a fire deep inside the mine, which could cause another explosion. They constantly checked the levels of carbon monoxide coming from the mine. Rising levels are signs of a fire. Unfortunately, the readings were so high that people had to begin evacuating buildings on the surface.

Near the mine entrance, the One Left crew watched in frustration. They wanted to rescue their fellow workers as quickly as possible. But officials felt that the risk to the rescue team was too great. They were not cleared to enter the mine until 5:30 p.m.—11 hours after the explosion.

WAITING FOR HELP

Inside the mine, the trapped miners were starting to wonder if rescue would ever come. Toler and another man had gone to look for a way out but returned quickly, gagging from the fumes. The miners gave up hammering on the bolts after several hours

with no response. And although their plastic curtain kept out smoke, it couldn't block all of the carbon monoxide. The men sat down and tried to stay still. They tried to breathe as shallowly as possible to conserve what oxygen was left. Many of the men began to pray. Some wrote messages to their loved ones. McCloy wrote a short note to his wife, telling her that he loved her. He put it in the lunchbox of one of the other miners, where he thought it was likely to be found.

Rescue workers wanted to help the miners, but their efforts were slowed by the poisonous gas in the mine.

RACE AGAINST TIME

Rescue teams were now in the mine, but they had to move slowly. They didn't want to trigger another explosion. They constantly tested for gases and weaknesses in the mine's roof. They also had to be careful with telephones and other electrical equipment. A single spark could cause a disaster. All these precautions meant that they could only move about 1,000 feet (300 m) per hour.

Twenty hours after the explosion, the rescuers had traveled 1.5 miles (2.4 km) into the mine. They were about halfway to the trapped miners. Above the surface, another team drilled a narrow hole down to where they thought the miners were. Gas level readings showed that the air was probably too bad for anyone to have survived.

Inside the barricade, McCloy was feeling more and more lightheaded. He watched in horror as some of his fellow miners drifted off into what looked like a deep sleep. One man collapsed to the ground, not moving. There was nothing McCloy could do to help. One by one, the others lost consciousness. McCloy was too weak to do anything but watch. The last thing he remembered was speaking to Jackie Weaver, who tried to provide words of comfort. Then McCloy passed out.

FATAL DISCOVERY

At about 5:00 p.m. on the day after the explosion, the rescue teams found debris in the mine. One man soon spotted a body. It was Terry Helms, the fire boss, who had been killed in the explosion. There was no sign of the other 12 men—they were deeper inside the mine.

Several crosses were set up in Phillippi, West Virginia, to honor the memory of the Sago Mine victims.

The rescuers kept moving forward. Finally, 40 hours after the explosion, they reached Two Left Section. One team set up a fresh air station, while the other group of six pushed on. As they entered the section, they found the empty cases for the Two Left crew's self-rescuers. This gave the rescuers hope that the miners might still be alive. Soon they approached the plastic curtain. One of the rescuers heard a moan, or possibly the wheeze of a man trying to breathe. They raced to pull away the curtain.

At first glance, it looked like the miners were sitting against the coalface. One rescuer shouted that they were alive. The men in the backup crew heard him. But the rescuers quickly realized that the miners were all dead—except for McCloy. He was unconscious and struggling to breathe.

MISUNDERSTANDINGS

Ron Hixson, one of the rescuers, sent a message. He said that all the miners had been found, one was still alive, and they needed help. But communications were patchy, and only the second part of the message got through. On the surface, people thought that all the miners had been found alive. Word quickly spread to the nearby church where the families were waiting. They erupted into celebrations. They hugged and screamed as the church bells rang. The governor of West Virginia prepared to go into the mine to meet the survivors as they emerged. It would be several hours before people learned the truth— McCloy was the only survivor.

MEDICAL CARE

McCloy was rushed to the hospital. He had severe carbon monoxide poisoning and had suffered a massive heart attack. He also had a collapsed lung, kidney failure, and extremely low blood pressure. He was in a deep coma as doctors raced to save his life. They worried that even if he pulled through, he could still have permanent brain damage.

The doctors transferred McCloy to a hospital in Pittsburgh, Pennsylvania. Doctors there put him in a hyperbaric chamber. This type of capsule has very high air pressure. It allows oxygen to penetrate a body's tissues, ridding it of carbon monoxide. The first treatment lasted 90 minutes, and during that time McCloy's condition got worse. The second treatment was slightly better. But during the third treatment, McCloy improved dramatically.

Randal McCloy spent several months in physical therapy to recover from his injuries in the Sago mine accident.

After three months in the hospital, McCloy was finally able to go home. Although he would eventually return to a normal life, he would never work in a mine again. "I done learned my lesson the hard way," he said.

EARTHQUAKE!
BRANT WEBB AND TODD RUSSELL

When gold was discovered in Tasmania in the 1800s, it sparked a gold rush. Prospectors raced to this small island nation south of Australia, hoping to strike it rich. Even more than 150 years later, mining gold and other metals continues to be one of Tasmania's most important industries. It's profitable, but it can also be dangerous.

GOING DOWN

On the evening of April 25, 2006, Brant Webb and Todd Russell entered the Beaconsfield gold mine to begin the night shift. It was Anzac Day, a national holiday to remember soldiers from Australia and New Zealand. While others celebrated, the two men stepped into an elevator to travel deep underground. The mine began with a long vertical shaft that plunged more than 1,000 feet (300 m) deep into the rock. Below that, a spiraling passageway went deeper into the earth. The level where Webb and Russell were working was 3,035 feet (925 m) below the surface.

The mine had experienced problems in the past. About six months earlier, there had been a rockfall in the level where the miners were working. That level had to be closed for several months before it could be reopened. The miners now used a new technique that they hoped would reduce the risk of another rockfall.

WORK BEGINS

That night Webb and Russell were working with a third miner, Larry Knight. They entered their level at about 7:30 p.m. Their job for the night was to build a retaining wall around an area that had recently been mined. Webb and Russell were working in a telehandler. This large machine had a telescoping arm with a mesh cage at the end. Webb and Russell were in the cage, while Knight was in the cabin, directing the machine.

At 9:23 p.m., an earthquake struck. It was fairly small—only about 2.3 on the Richter scale. But it was big enough to cause a significant rock fall. About 880 tons (800 metric tons) of rock and rubble fell onto the telehandler. People all over the town felt the earthquake. Fourteen miners were able to scramble to safety. But the men working 3,035 feet (925 m) below the surface were missing.

WAKING IN THE DARK

The moment before the earthquake hit, Russell had been about to take a drink of water. The next thing he remembers is that it was pitch dark, and they were covered in rock. "It happened quicker than what you could blink," he said later.

Russell's legs were buried in rock, and Webb had been knocked unconscious. There was no sign of Knight. Webb soon woke up, and he pulled a cigarette lighter from his pocket to get some light. When he clicked it, the truth of the situation hit him hard. "Those first 15 seconds were the most horrific 15 seconds of my life," he recalled. The metal cage had saved them, but they were completely buried in rock, deep underground.

The rocks covering Russell's lower body were slowly crushing him. Webb managed to dig him out, but he had no way to treat his coworker's leg injuries. The two men were trapped in complete darkness, in a space only 4 feet (0.4 m) square. They had no food other than a single granola bar in Webb's pocket. Luckily, water was seeping through the rock. They collected it in their helmets to drink.

RESCUE ATTEMPTS

The upper levels of the mine were fairly clear. Rescuers used a remote-controlled vehicle to try to reach the place where the three men had been working. Nearly 36 hours after the earthquake, they found Knight's body. The falling rocks had killed him. Many of the rescuers feared that Webb and Russell were also dead. The constant risk of rockfall meant that they needed to find a different way to reach Webb and Russell. They began to blast a new tunnel.

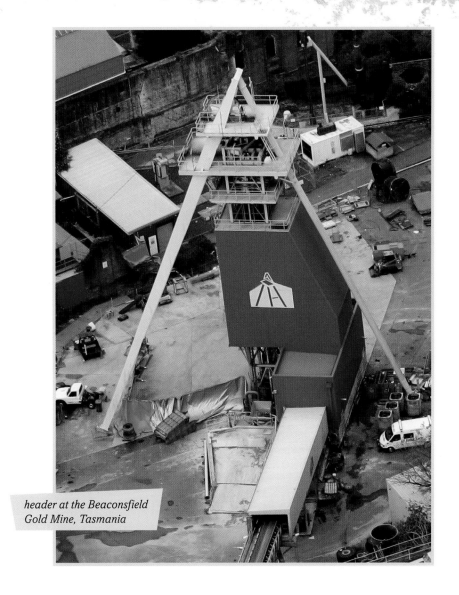

header at the Beaconsfield Gold Mine, Tasmania

The two men could feel the blasts of rescuers working on a new tunnel. Each blast dislodged more rock. They worried that the massive weight of rock above them would eventually fall and crush them. They had no paper, so they wrote messages to their families on their clothes. They still had hope of being rescued. But they tried to mentally prepare themselves for the worst.

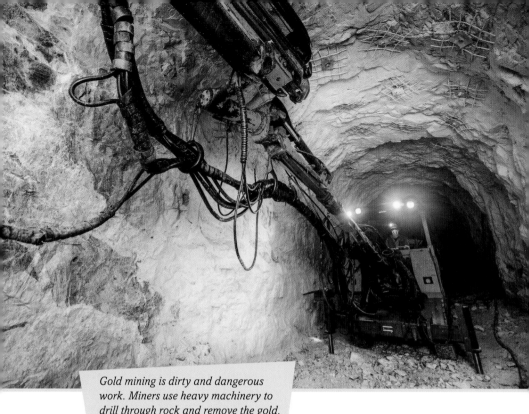

Gold mining is dirty and dangerous work. Miners use heavy machinery to drill through rock and remove the gold.

DID YOU KNOW?

Rescuers also delivered music players loaded with music that Webb and Russell had requested. One of Webb's requests was for music by the Foo Fighters. The band's leader, Dave Grohl, heard about the request and was touched. He sent a message to the survivors. It said, "My heart is with you both. I want you to know that when you come home, there's two tickets to any Foos show, anywhere . . . waiting for you."

FOUND!

By the evening of April 30, Webb and Russell had been trapped for nearly five full days. Their families and co-workers had no idea whether they were still alive. To keep their spirits up, the two men sang together. They chose "The Gambler" by Kenny Rogers. It was the only song to which they both knew the words. Then they heard a sound that was truly music to their ears—the shout of a rescue worker.

Webb and Russell yelled back, as loudly as they could. They had finally been found! The rescue team's first job was to get them supplies. By the next day they had drilled a narrow tunnel to the cage. It was only 3.5 inches (9 cm) in diameter. But it was big enough to send fresh water, liquid food, and medical supplies through a pipe.

A LONG, HARD TASK

Digging the two men out would be difficult. Rescue workers couldn't just remove the rubble that had fallen—it was too unstable. Instead, they began drilling a new tunnel. It traveled horizontally, below the level where Webb and Russell were buried. Once the tunnel reached their location, they planned to start drilling upward. They would reach the men from below. Rescuers hoped that this method would avoid dislodging the rocks above the men.

FEELING BETTER

It was no fun being trapped in a space too small to move around. But at least the two men had food, water, and hope of rescue. A telephone had been installed, and they could speak to paramedics. They also wrote and received letters from their families. Contact with the outside world helped keep them feeling positive.

SLOW PROGRESS

The rescue team brought in a drilling machine that could bore a hole 39 inches (1 m) wide. But they first had to wait until the machine's concrete anchor had set hard. It was late on May 3 before they began. They had to cut through about 40 feet (12 m) of solid rock before they could start drilling upward. The drill was capable of cutting 39 inches (1 m) per hour, but they went at half that speed. They didn't want to risk causing another rockfall.

By May 8, the rescue team was getting close. The drilling machine had finished the horizontal tunnel. Now they could start digging up toward Webb and Russell. But the rock was incredibly hard, and their jackhammers couldn't break through. They would need to use explosives. This was a risky option that was seen as a last resort.

Luckily, Darren Flanagan had flown in from the mainland to help. He was an expert in a new technique of using low-impact explosives. For several days he had been conducting test explosions in a higher level of the mine. He was trying to create the perfect blast—one that wouldn't cause too many dangerous vibrations.

3, 2, 1, FIRE!

Now was the time for the real blast. Flanagan crawled into the tunnel with his equipment. Before he started, he spoke to Webb and Russell on the telephone. He explained that there would be a lot of noise, but very little vibration. The trapped miners knew that any explosion could cause further collapse. But they also knew it was the only way for rescuers to reach them. They told Flanagan to start blasting.

Explosives expert Darren Flanagan

In the end, it took 29 hours and 65 separate blasts. Each one blew away a little more of the rock separating the rescuers from the miners. Before each blast, Flanagan and the two men would count down together: "3, 2, 1, fire!" Flanagan stopped blasting once he had reached a spot just 12 inches (30 cm) from the men's location. Other rescuers then used hand tools to break through to the cage.

After 14 days trapped underground, Todd Russell (left) and Brant Webb (center) had become famous. They waved to the cheering crowd after being rescued.

FREE AT LAST

Freedom finally came at 4:47 a.m. on May 9. Webb and Russell had been trapped in their tiny cage for two weeks! Rescue workers helped them through the narrow tunnel. They were driven up through the mine until they reached an underground medical station. Doctors checked them over, and the men each had a shower and changed into clean clothes.

During their time underground, crowds and camera crews had gathered around the mine entrance. When Webb and Russell emerged from the elevator, they were greeted with huge cheers. The two men pumped their fists in the air and walked over to the safety board. They took their tags off the board and moved them to the "safe" position, signaling that they had finished their shift. It had been the longest shift of their lives!

Webb and Russell were overjoyed to be reunited with their families. Ambulances were waiting to take them to the hospital. Despite their ordeal, neither man was badly hurt. They had injuries to their knees and backs, but nothing too serious. Russell was released within a few hours, just in time to attend Larry Knight's funeral.

CELEBRITY

Webb and Russell tried to return to a normal life, but everyone in Australia wanted to hear their story. They were interviewed on television and in newspapers. A few months later, the Foo Fighters were playing in Sydney, Australia, and Webb accepted Dave Grohl's offer of free tickets. Afterward, Grohl was inspired to write a song called "Ballad of the Beaconsfield Miners." It appeared on the band's next album.

The people of Tasmania won't forget the story of this amazing rescue. In 2012 a movie about the rescue was shown on Australian television. Just a few months later, the Beaconsfield mine closed. It was no longer making a profit. Today the mine has been turned into a museum, showcasing the history of mining in Tasmania. It's no surprise that one of its most popular exhibits is about Webb and Russell's rescue!

69 DAYS
THE CHILEAN MINERS

Riches are hidden beneath South America's Andes Mountains. These tall mountains snake down the western edge of the continent. The rocks that form the mountains contain iron, gold, silver, tin, and other useful minerals. The San José Mine, in northern Chile, produced small amounts of gold, but its main product was copper.

THE SHIFT BEGINS

On the morning of August 5, 2010, the "A" crew arrived at the mine for their 12-hour shift. Some of the men lived in the nearby city of Copiapó. Others traveled long distances—sometimes several hundred miles—to get to work. Working at the mine paid well. Even the lowest-paid workers at San José earned more than three times the minimum wage in Chile. The trade-off for this was that the work was hard, dusty—and sometimes dangerous. The San José Mine didn't have a spotless safety record.

As the miners gathered at the entrance, they met the night shift on their way out. These tired and dusty men told them that the mountain was "weeping" a lot. This was their way of saying that they'd heard a lot of rumbling, as rocks fell in empty pockets deep inside the mountain.

The men had heard this type of rumbling before. It usually stopped eventually. So the "A" crew climbed into a truck for the long drive to their workplace. The San José mine cuts deep into the mountain. Instead of a vertical shaft, a long tunnel called the Ramp spirals down. The Ramp was big enough for trucks and heavy machinery to drive on it. It took 40 minutes to drive about 3 miles (5 km) down to the bottom of the mine.

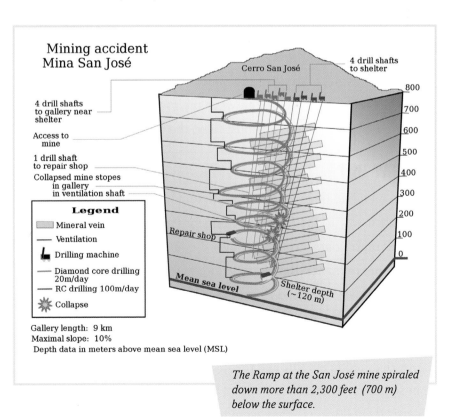

The Ramp at the San José mine spiraled down more than 2,300 feet (700 m) below the surface.

DISASTER STRIKES

As the miners worked, some of them began to feel uneasy. The mountain was definitely noisy today—noisier than usual. Some of the men wanted to stop work and return to the surface. But the manager decided not to close the mine. Shortly after 1:00 p.m., Franklin Lobos began the long drive down to collect the men for lunch. He had nearly reached them when there was a massive explosion, and the passageway around him filled with dust.

COLLAPSE

A huge block of rock, the height of a 45-story building, had broken loose from the rest of the mountain. It fell downward, smashing through the Ramp as it went. It pulled stones loose as it fell, creating shockwaves that made the whole mine shake.

Amazingly, many of the men working in the mine didn't hear the collapse. Many of them were in levels that branched off from the Ramp. They wore ear protection and were operating loud, heavy machinery. Even so, some of the miners felt a squeezing sensation. It was the result of the pressure wave the rock collapse had triggered. Soon choking rock dust filled the tunnels.

NO WAY OUT

The men had been working in different areas, but now they all made their way to the Ramp, heading for the exit. Many of them climbed onto Lobos' truck, and they drove slowly through the dust. As they drove higher, they found more and more debris in their path. Eventually they had to get out and walk.

Then the men's headlamps lit up a grey stone slab that blocked the Ramp completely. The wall of rock was the side of the huge block that had fallen through the mountain. The miners stared at it in shocked silence. This wasn't a simple rockfall that could be cleared by bulldozers. They were trapped.

WHAT TO DO?

On the surface, the first sign something was wrong was the thick cloud of dust billowing from the mine entrance. Rescue workers drove into the mine to see if they could reach the men below. As they went, they saw numerous cracks in the walls, ceiling, and floor. Eventually they encountered a solid mass of rock blocking the path.

The rescue workers knew that 33 men were still in the mine. Some of them tried to rappel down the ventilation shafts that plunged deep into the mine. They hoped to reach a level below the collapse, where the miners might be still alive. But soon another collapse crushed the ventilation shafts. They would have to find another way inside.

DRILLING DOWN

The only way to get the men out was by drilling through solid rock. Even if they could be found alive, rescuing them could take weeks. Rescuers brought in high-speed drilling rigs to drill exploratory holes, each about 6 inches (15 cm) wide. They hoped the holes would lead to signs of life.

After realizing there was no way out, the miners gathered in a chamber called the Refuge. It was designed as an emergency shelter. It had a small stock of food and water, and fresh air was pumped in from the surface. The room was about 540 square feet (50 square m). The men quickly found that all communication with the surface had been knocked out by the rock collapse. There was also no electricity, water, compressed air, or intercom.

TAKING CHARGE

The shift supervisor, Luis Urzúa, took charge of the situation. The men naturally looked up to him. Urzúa organized a system for rationing the miners' food supply. The men got only a spoonful of canned tuna and a few sips of milk each day. Over the next two weeks, he drew maps and planned out areas for sleeping, working, and washing. He made work schedules and kept everyone calm.

On August 22, one of the boreholes finally broke through into an area near the Refuge. At this point the miners had been trapped for 17 days. They taped a message to the drill bit that read *"Estamos bien en el Refugio los 33* (The 33 of us are well in the Refuge)." When this message arrived at the surface, the gathered crowds cheered. It was the first evidence that the miners had survived.

MAKING A PLAN

The miners had been found alive, but how would they get out? There was no way of digging through the blockage in the Ramp. The rescuers would have to drill down through thousands of feet of solid rock. Then they could send down an escape capsule to bring the miners up, one by one. On the surface, rescue teams gathered the heavy drilling machines and other equipment they would need to reach the trapped miners.

IN THE DEPTHS

The miners' health was an immediate concern. Rescuers could send supplies down previously drilled boreholes in long, thin canisters. But the 33 men had hardly eaten for 17 days. Eating too much, too soon, could kill them. With advice from NASA scientists, doctors sent down special energy gels and drinks.

The rescue teams then set up a phone line and sent down video cameras. They discovered that the miners were in good health and spirits, considering what they had been through. The trapped miners could exchange letters with their families. But they knew that it might be months before the rescuers reached them.

After a borehole broke through, workers lowered a video camera to see the miners. The blurry video showed that the men were dirty, thin, and shirtless, but mostly healthy.

DAILY LIFE

It was important for the miners to keep busy and try to live as normally as possible. It kept them from worrying too much or getting depressed. Led by Urzúa, the men soon fell into a routine. Every morning one of the first jobs was to unpack the breakfast delivery. After eating, the men cleaned the living area and took a shower in a natural waterfall.

They then split up to do different jobs. One man was in charge of checking the air quality, while others reinforced walls or checked for signs of further rock falls. After lunch, the men would gather for a meeting and vote on any issues. Then they relaxed for a few hours. At night they could sleep on air mattresses sent down in the supply capsules.

The miners had been found, but they were still in a very difficult situation. The mine was hot and very humid, with temperatures that could reach over 100 °F (38 °C). At least the miners had electricity and water, plus a regular food supply. They also had plenty of space, with more than 1 mile (1.6 km) of unblocked tunnels.

DID YOU KNOW?

Some of the men naturally took on new roles. José Henríquez organized daily prayer sessions. Mario Sepúlveda made video journals to send to the surface. Yonni Barrios, who had a bit of medical training, became the group's medic. Doctors on the surface gave him help and advice.

The T 130 drilling machine dug the closest hole to the location of the trapped miners.

THREE PLANS

Rescue workers planned to drill three rescue holes, using three different machines. That way, if a machine failed or the shaft collapsed, they'd still have two other options. Plan A used a driller that was powerful but slow. It would take months to get down to the miners. Plan B would use a machine that used hammers to smash through the rock more quickly. It would widen one of the boreholes used for sending supplies. Plan C was a powerful oil-drilling rig, but it didn't start drilling until September 19.

Drilling machines require huge amounts of water for cooling and lubrication. Unfortunately, the mine was in the middle of the Atacama desert—one of the driest places on Earth. The nearest water source was a well about an hour's drive away. A constant stream of tanker trucks drove back and forth to bring water.

All three machines had problems drilling through the hard rock. Drill bits broke and engines failed. Engineers and mechanics labored around the clock to keep the machines working. Deep in the mine, the 33 trapped men were getting frustrated at the delays.

ESCAPE CAPSULES

Meanwhile, engineers were designing a way to pull up the miners once the drills reached them. They needed a capsule that could hold a man but was only 21 inches (54 cm) in diameter. NASA engineers worked with the Chilean navy to design a capsule that they called the Fénix, or Phoenix. It had a light and an oxygen supply, as well as a video communication system. There was also an escape hatch at the bottom, in case the capsule got stuck.

The Plan B machine reached the miners on September 17, 43 days into their ordeal. But this hole was only 12 inches (30 cm) wide. Now they had to drill again with a bigger bit to widen the hole enough for the Fénix. It took the machine 21 days to widen the hole. It sent several tons of debris down into the mine each day, which the trapped miners had to clear away.

SUCCESS!

As the drill got closer, operators slowed it down. They didn't want to risk another rockfall. Finally, at 8:05 a.m. on October 9, they broke through. There were huge cheers both above and below ground. The miners' families, who had been camped near the mine entrance for two months, knew they would be seeing their loved ones soon.

However, the men couldn't be brought up right away. Engineers inspected the borehole to see if it needed to be supported with steel pipes. This would eliminate the risk of rocks falling and jamming the lifting equipment. Then they had to pour a concrete platform for the Fénix's winch. Finally, everything had to be tested.

The Fénix finally went into operation on October 12. A rescue worker, Manuel González, climbed in and was sent down. He helped the first miner, Florencio Avalos, strap into the capsule. At 12:11 a.m. on October 13, Avalos reached the surface. Although it was night, he wore sunglasses. After 69 days underground, he needed to protect his eyes from the bright lights. The rest of the miners followed, one by one. Each round-trip took about an hour. Luis Urzúa was the last to emerge. Chile's president, Sebastián Piñera, was on hand to greet each man as he came out.

The trapped miners had to ride one by one in the rescue capsule to reach the surface.

Jimmy Sanchez was the fifth miner to ride to safety in the Fenix rescue capsule. The miners had to wear sunglasses after being trapped underground for more than two months.

BACK TO REALITY

More than a billion people around the world watched the live TV broadcast of the rescue. For 69 days, the story had been covered in every corner of the globe. The videos sent up by the miners made viewers feel as if they knew them. Everyone had been hoping for success, and now they wanted to hear from these amazing survivors. Journalists wrote books about the rescue, and several documentaries were produced. In 2015, the Hollywood film *The 33* told their story, starring Antonio Banderas as Mario Sepúlveda.

The miners had been saved, but the accident raised serious questions about mine safety. Mine owners had cut corners to save on costs, but this would now stop. Government officials shut down 18 other mines soon after the collapse.

Today the 'Fénix' capsule is displayed at the Regional Museum of Atacama in Copiapo, Chile.

DIVING INTO DARKNESS
XISCO GRÀCIA LLADÓUN

Winding, twisting cave systems are found in many parts of the world. Their networks of connected tunnels and chambers can stretch for miles. These caverns are often glittering with mineral deposits and stalactites, creating an irresistible lure for cavers. But exploring these underground jewels can be dangerous. The caves often have tight spaces to squeeze through, and it's easy to get lost. Finding a way through these underground passages is even more difficult when they're filled with water. Cave divers use scuba gear to explore deep, water-filled caves. It's an extreme sport that can sometimes turn deadly.

MAPPING AND EXPLORING

Xisco Gràcia Lladóun is from the Spanish island of Mallorca. The land is criss-crossed with caves. Some are above sea level. But others are lower and filled with water. Gràcia is a geology teacher who loves nothing more than suiting up to explore and map the caves. He once said that he thought Mallorca was more beautiful below the ground than above! For 20 years, he had been slowly adding to scientists' knowledge about the caves.

On April 15, 2017, Gràcia and his friend, Guillem Mascaró, prepared to go on a long dive. The two 54-year-olds wanted to explore a cave called Sa Piqueta. About 0.6 miles (1 km) from the entrance was a series of chambers that had never been studied. This was their target.

BE PREPARED!

Both men were experienced cave divers. They knew how dangerous it could be. The two men checked and rechecked their equipment before entering the cave. They had calculated how long they would be underwater. Gràcia made sure to take more bottled air than they would need, in case of emergencies. He had four extra bottles clipped to his dive belt, and Mascaró had three. The two cave divers carried a coil of thin nylon rope. They would stretch the rope out behind them as they swam. If needed, they could follow this guideline to find their way out of the caves. They also had flashlights, cameras, and tools for taking rock samples.

GOING IN

It took Gràcia and Mascaró about an hour to swim to the chambers they wanted to explore. As they went, they carefully set down their guideline. The path twisted and forked many times. Each time it split, they set a numbered marker. Then they laid a guideline on the new path. It took time to set down this system of rope, labels, and arrows. But it was important to do it right.

The water in the narrow passages was clear, but as they swam, the two men kicked up sediment from the bottom. This sediment would take hours to settle again, and it could reduce visibility to practically zero. In conditions like that, the divers would have to feel their way out, blindly following the guideline.

Cave divers lay down guidelines to help them find their way back when exploring uncharted underwater caves.

CHARTING NEW GROUND

The underground chambers were everything that Gràcia had hoped. He loved being the first to explore new caves. He took rock samples while Mascaró swam into the next chamber to take measurements. Later they planned to use those measurements to fill in some blank spaces on the cave map.

After they had explored for about an hour, Gràcia checked the gauge on his air tanks. They each had 2 to 2.5 hours of air left. It had taken them about an hour to travel this far into the cave. So they had about an hour left to explore before heading back. Gràcia was experienced enough to know that divers should always leave extra air in case of emergencies.

AN UNFORESEEN PROBLEM

When it was time to leave, the divers began the long swim back. But the water was already muddy. The men followed the guideline hand over hand. The water got even muddier as their air tanks scraped against the walls of the narrow passages. "It was like diving in a bowl of cacao [cocoa]," Gràcia later described it.

They were making good progress, but then disaster struck. Gràcia was in the lead, and he came to a rock wall where the guideline suddenly ended! He felt for the next section of the line, but he couldn't find it. Perhaps the rock it was tied to had broken off, or maybe a rock fall had snapped it.

Without guidelines to follow, cave divers can quickly get lost the the murky depths.

LOST!

Whatever the reason for the guideline's disappearance, the results were the same. Gràcia and Mascaró didn't know which way to swim to reach the cave entrance. Increasingly fearful, they searched for the line. By the time they gave up, they had used much of their extra air. Even if they knew the way, they would probably run out before they reached the surface.

It was every cave diver's worst nightmare. Luckily, Gràcia knew that about 660 feet (200 m) back, there was a cavern with a high ceiling. The men would have air to breathe there while they decided what to do. The two men swam back and hauled themselves out of the water. They found themselves in a large chamber, about 262 feet (80 m) long and 66 feet (20 m) wide. Around the lake they had just emerged from, pointed rocks reached high above the water's surface.

SAFE . . . FOR THE MOMENT

Gràcia knew that the air in the cavern would have more carbon dioxide than normal air. But as he removed his regulator and took a deep breath, his heart sank. The air had even higher levels of carbon dioxide than he'd expected. A person could only survive in air like that for a limited time.

The two divers examined their map. There was another path out of the cave, which was longer than the way they had entered. It had a guideline, but only for part of the route. And there was only enough air left in their tanks for one person to get out. One of them would have to stay behind and wait for the other to bring a rescue team.

After a discussion, the two men decided that Mascaró would swim for help. He didn't want to leave his friend behind, but Gràcia pointed out that Mascaró was smaller, faster, and would need less air. Gràcia had more experience breathing cave air. He thought that he would be able to survive longer in the cavern.

DID YOU KNOW?

The air in caves is often high in carbon dioxide. Water dripping down into the caves releases the gas. Dead plants and animals breaking down also can produce it. Trapped in a cave, the gas builds up over time. Carbon dioxide is heavier than the other gases in the air. It often forms pockets near the bottoms of open cave spaces.

ALL ALONE

Gràcia helped his friend clip on the remaining air tanks, and then watched as Mascaró disappeared below the surface of the water. Now he was on his own in the dark. How long would it take for rescuers to arrive? He took off the rest of his equipment and briefly explored the cavern. He discovered that the water at the surface of the lake was drinkable. He also found a flat rock where he could haul himself out of the water. Staying too long in the cold water would lead to hypothermia—a dangerous condition when a person's body temperature drops too low.

Out of Gràcia's three flashlights, only one still worked, and its batteries were running low. Gràcia turned it off to save the batteries. He lay down and concentrated on taking slow, shallow breaths. This would keep him from taking in too much carbon dioxide. But he could already feel his pulse quickening. He knew this was an early sign of carbon dioxide poisoning.

WAITING AND WORRYING

The hours passed slowly as Gràcia waited for rescuers to arrive. At first, he was fairly hopeful that help would come. But after seven or eight hours in the dark, he began to worry. Mascaró didn't know the caves as well as he did. He might have gotten lost. What if he hadn't managed to make it to the surface before his air ran out?

No one else knew where Gràcia was. Without Mascaró to give his location, no one would be able to find him. Meanwhile, the carbon dioxide was beginning to have serious effects. Gràcia had a headache and felt exhausted. But the thoughts running through his brain made it impossible to sleep.

Gràcia had only one working flashlight in the dark cave.

ON THE SURFACE

Despite Gràcia's fears, Mascaró made it out. He had swum desperately, reaching the other cave entrance in less than an hour. After sucking in several deep breaths of fresh air, he called Mallorca's official caving organization.

By now it was early evening, but as darkness fell, a rescue team of experienced cave divers gathered. One of them was Gràcia's friend Bernat Clamor. He knew that the cave had high levels of carbon dioxide. If they wanted to save Gràcia, they had to get him out quickly.

Two divers who were familiar with the cave system went in first. But they were back within two hours. In his frantic haste to reach the surface, Mascaró had kicked up a lot of sediment. With visibility at almost zero, the rescue divers couldn't find Gràcia. Clamor made the difficult decision to call a stop. It would take several hours for the sediment to settle before they could try again. Gràcia might already be running out of air.

TIME RUNNING OUT

Deep in the cavern, Gràcia didn't know how long he had been alone. His watch had stopped, and he felt dizzy from the carbon dioxide building up in his body. The more carbon dioxide a person breathes in, the less oxygen one's body can absorb. Along with dizziness and headaches, symptoms of carbon dioxide poisoning include nausea, sweating, and confusion.

Alone in the darkness, Gràcia became convinced that Mascaró had died trying to get out. He thought about what would happen to his children if he didn't make it out alive. He even began to hallucinate, imagining that he saw lights and heard bubbles in the water.

He had decided earlier to stay as still as possible, moving only to drink or urinate. But now Gràcia decided to swim across to where he had left his gear. He wanted to retrieve his knife. He knew he was facing a slow death from lack of food and air. "I wanted to have it as a last resort if I needed to choose whether to die quickly or slowly," he explained later.

Mascaró rushed back to the cave entrance to get help for his friend.

RESCUE ATTEMPTS CONTINUE

At the surface, the rescue divers were still waiting for the water to clear. They tried to drill down to the cavern where Gràcia was slowly suffocating. They hoped that they could send food and oxygen down the hole, but they were unable to reach the cavern. By this point Gràcia had been there for more than 30 hours. A team of more than 60 people was waiting to help, but they could do nothing until the water was clearer.

After an agonizing 15-hour wait, the divers tried again. It took the first man two hours to cut all the guidelines except the ones that led to Gràcia's cavern. Then it was Clamor's turn. He followed the remaining guideline until he reached his goal.

Some caves in Mallorca, such as the famous "Dragon Caves," are safer and easier to explore. They are a popular tourist attraction.

SAFE AT LAST!

In his confused state, Gràcia thought it was another hallucination when he saw lights and heard bubbles. But then he saw Clamor emerging from the water. The two friends hugged, and Clamor told him that Mascaró had survived. He also gave Gràcia some oxygen and energy gel before leaving to alert the rescuers.

The next divers brought extra tanks full of nitrox—a gas with twice as much oxygen as regular air. As he breathed it, Gràcia's head started to clear. He began to feel stronger. Despite his weakened state, he would still have a long swim to safety. His fellow divers slowly led him up to the surface. By the time he emerged and was reunited with Mascaró, he had been underground for more than 60 hours.

BACK TO WORK

Gràcia was taken to the hospital and given pure oxygen to breathe. By the following morning, he was well enough to go home to recover. But there was no way he was going to give up his favorite hobby! Just a month after his terrifying ordeal, he was back in Sa Piqueta. He was given the honor of choosing a name for the cavern where he had waited so long. He decided to call it "The Room of the Three Miracles." He felt that he had experienced three miracles: finding a chamber with air, surviving the carbon dioxide for so long, and escaping with his life.

GLOSSARY

air pressure—the weight of air pushing against something

backhoe—a digging machine with a bucket at the end of a long arm

barricade—something put up to block a passage and stop someone or something from getting in

carbon dioxide—a colorless, odorless gas found in the air; people and animals make carbon dioxide as a waste product.

carbon monoxide—a poisonous gas produced when substances containing carbon burn

coma—a state of deep unconsciousness from which it is very hard to wake up

energy gel—a thick, sugar-based liquid often used by athletes to provide quick energy

flammable—likely to catch fire

gangrene—a condition in which body tissues die from lack of blood supply

hallucination—an experience of seeing or hearing something that is not really there

hypothermia—a life-threatening condition that occurs when a person's core body temperature falls several degrees below normal

jackhammer—a handheld tool that uses compressed air to drill through rock or concrete

oxygen—a colorless gas that people and animals need to breathe to survive

paramedic—a medical professional trained to provide emergency care

prospector—a person who explores an area for valuable minerals, especially silver and gold

rappel—to descend a steep surface using a rope coiled around the body and attached at a higher point

sediment—tiny particles of rock, sand, or mud that are carried along by water and eventually settle at the bottom

stalactite—a growth of rock that hangs from the roof of a cave and is formed by dripping water

vibration—a fast movement back and forth

READ MORE

Aronson, Mark. *Trapped: How the World Rescued 33 Miners from 2,000 Feet Below the Chilean Desert.* New York: Atheneum Books for Young Readers, 2019.

Garrison, Hal. *Cave Diving.* New York: Gareth Stevens, 2018.

Lewis, Mark L. *Underground Rescues.* Lake Elmo, MN: Focus Readers, 2020.

Peter, Carsten. *Extreme Planet: Carsten Peter's Adventures in Volcanoes, Caves, Canyons, Deserts, and Beyond!* Washington, D.C.: National Geographic, 2015.

INTERNET SITES

2010 Chilean Mine Rescue Fast Facts
https://edition.cnn.com/2013/07/13/world/americas/chilean-mine-rescue/index.html

Baby Jessica Biography
https://www.biography.com/personality/baby-jessica

Beaconsfield Gold Mine
http://www.tasmanianlife.com.au/beaconsfield/

Coal Mining Facts
https://kids.kiddle.co/Coal_mining

SOURCE NOTES

p. 7, "I didn't know what to do…" Lianne Hart and Anne Maier, "The Epic Rescue of Jessica McClure," *People*, November 2, 1987, https://people.com/archive/cover-story-the-epic-rescue-of-jessica-mcclure-vol-28-no-18/. Accessed June 29, 2019.

p. 13, "For Jessica 10-16-87, with love from all of us." "Baby Jessica: 30 Years Later," https://www.peopleewnetwork.com/video/baby-jessica-30-years-later-170309-pen-peoplefeat-207-v03, Accessed June 29, 2019.

p. 25, "I done learned my lesson the hard way." AP interview with Randal McCloy, March 29, 2006, https://www.youtube.com/watch?v=6Y3AXWz4dAw (approximately 2:30). Accessed June 29, 2019.

p. 28, "It happened quicker than what you could blink." Magistrate's report on the inquest on the death of Larry Paul Knight, http://www.mineaccidents.com.au/uploads/beaconsfield-original.pdf. Accessed June 29, 2019.

p. 28, "Those first 15 seconds were the most horrific 15 seconds of my life." *60 Minutes: Beaconsfield Mine Disaster: 10 Years On*, 2016, https://www.youtube.com/watch?reload=9&v=GUFL6P2Ap2I (approximately 4:20). Accessed June 29, 2019.

p. 31, "My heart is with you both." https://www.songfacts.com/facts/foo-fighters/ballad-of-the-beaconsfield-miners. Accessed June 29, 2019.

p. 33, "3, 2, 1, fire!" Channel 10 news report, May 9, 2006, https://www.youtube.com/watch?v=hhN0SMr1RXE (approximately 2:20). Accessed June 29, 2019.

p. 41, "Estamos bien en el Refugio los 33." Antonio de la Jara and Simon Gardner. "Trapped Chile miners alive but long rescue ahead," *Reuters*, August 22, 2010. Accessed June 29, 2019.

p. 51, "It was like diving in a bowl of cacao." Marissa Payne, "'I was buried alive: Diver survives 60 hours trapped in an underwater cave," *Washington Post*, July 22, 2017, https://www.washingtonpost.com/news/early-lead/wp/2017/07/22/i-was-buried-alive-diver-survives-60-hours-trapped-in-an-underwater-cave. Accessed June 29, 2019.

p. 57, "I wanted to have it as a last resort…" Claire Bates, "Two days in an underwater cave running out of oxygen," BBC World Service, July 17, 2017, https://www.bbc.co.uk/news/magazine-40558067. Accessed June 29, 2019.

BIBLIOGRAPHY

Books

Tobar, Hector. *Deep Down Dark: The Untold Stories of the 33 Men Buried in a Chilean Mine and the Miracle That Set Them Free*. Sceptre, 2014.

Websites and Articles

"2010 Chilean Mine Rescue Fast Facts," *CNN Library*, April 22, 2019, https://edition.cnn.com/2013/07/13/world/americas/chilean-mine-rescue/index.html. Accessed June 29, 2019.

"Baby Jessica: 30 Years Later," *People TV*, https://www.peopleewnetwork.com/video/baby-jessica-30-years-later-170309-pen-peoplefeat-207-v03. Accessed June 29, 2019.

Bates, Claire. "Two Days In An Underwater Cave Running Out of Oxygen," *BBC News*, July 17, 2017, https://www.bbc.co.uk/news/magazine-40558067. Accessed June 29, 2017.

"Beaconsfield Mine Disaster—10 Years On," *60 Minutes*, August 9, 2016, https://www.youtube.com/watch?v=GUFL6P2Ap2I. Accessed June 29, 2019.

Grainger, Lia. "These Two Cave Divers Were Trapped Underwater—with Only Enough Oxygen for One," *Reader's Digest*, https://www.rd.com/true-stories/survival/cave-divers-trapped-underwater/. Accessed June 29, 2019.

Hart, Lianne and Anne Maier. "The Epic Rescue of Jessica McClure," *People*, November 2, 1987, https://people.com/archive/cover-story-the-epic-rescue-of-jessica-mcclure-vol-28-no-18/. Accessed June 29, 2019.

Magistrates Court of Tasmania, Coronial Division. "In the Matter of the Coroners Act 1995 and In the Matter of an Inquest Touching the Death of Larry Paul Knight." February 26, 2009, http://www.mineaccidents.com.au/uploads/beaconsfield-original.pdf. Accessed June 29, 2019.

"Rescued Miner McCloy Speaks Out for First Time," *Today*, March 30, 2006, https://www.today.com/news/rescued-miner-mccloy-speaks-out-first-time-wbna12072995. Accessed June 29, 2019.

"Sago Mine Disaster," *Discovery Times*, January 3, 2015, https://www.youtube.com/watch?v=IGb20ZDbjkY. Accessed June 29, 2019.

INDEX

ABOUT THE AUTHOR

Nancy Dickmann has written more than 150 nonfiction books for children, specializing in science and history. Before becoming an author, she worked for many years as an editor and publisher of children's books.